OH LORD I PRAY

A DAILY WALK IN FAITH THROUGH PRAYER

Jan Keegan

Author's Tranquility Press
ATLANTA, GEORGIA

Copyright © 2025 by Jan Keegan

All rights reserved. No part of this publication may be reproduced, distributed or transmitted in any form or by any means, including photocopying, recording, or other electronic or mechanical methods, without the prior written permission of the publisher, except in the case of brief quotations embodied in critical reviews and certain other noncommercial uses permitted by copyright law. For permission requests, write to the publisher, addressed "Attention: Permissions Coordinator," at the address below.

All scriptures used in these writings come from the NEW REVISED STANDARD VERSION of the BIBLE.

Art and Design Illustration by Heather H. Hatheway

Jan Keegan/Author's Tranquility Press
3900 N Commerce Dr. Suite 300 #1255
Atlanta, GA 30344, USA
www.authorstranquilitypress.com

Ordering Information:
Quantity sales. Special discounts are available on quantity purchases by corporations, associations, and others. For details, contact the "Special Sales Department" at the address above.

Library of Congress Control Number: 2024924399

ISBN
Oh Lord I Pray / Jan Keegan
Hardback: 978-1-965463-50-5
Paperback: 978-1-965463-20-8
eBook: 978-1-965463-21-5

"Before they call, I will answer, while they are yet speaking, I will hear."

-Isaiah 65, verse 14 NRSV

For My Grandmother,
Charlotte Morris

Table of Contents

BIBLICAL SCRIPTURE ON PRAYER vi
PREFACE viii
Day 1 Guidance and Direction 1
Day 2 Love and Compassion 2
Day 3 Serving God 3
Day 4 Closeness to God 4
Day 5 Comfort and Contentment 5
Day 6 Acceptance 6
Day 7 Cleansing of My Soul 7
Day 8 Thankfulness 8
Day 9 Knowledge and Wisdom 9
Day 10 Almighty 10
Day 11 Restoration 11
Day 12 Peacemaker... 12
Day 13 Healing of My Soul 13
Day 14 Strength 14
Day 15 Understanding 15
Day 16 Encouragement 16
Day 17 Surroundings 17
Day 18 Spirituality 18
Day 19 Meditation 19
Day 20 The Will of God 20
Day 21 Everlasting Light 21
Day 22 The Presence of God 22
Day 23 Temptation 23
Day 24 Pray for Others 24
Day 25 Trust in God 25
Day 26 Faith 26
Day 27 Sin 27
Day 28 Glorify God 28
Day 29 Inclusive Prayer 29
Day 30 Self 30
Day 31 Humbleness 31

BIBLICAL SCRIPTURE ON PRAYER

"In the morning, while it was still very dark, he got up and went out to a deserted place, and there he prayed." Mark 1: 35. NRSV

"Jesus, Our Lord said, 'Pray then in this way: Our Father in heaven, hallowed be your name. your kingdom come. your will be done, on earth as it is in heaven. Give us this day our daily bread. And forgive us our debts, as we forgive our debtors. And do not bring us to the time of trial, but rescue us from the evil one.'" Matthew 6: 9-13 NRSV

"Jesus, Our Lord said, 'But whenever you pray, go into your room and shut the door and pray to your Father who is in secret; and your Father who sees in secret will reward you.'" Matthew 6:6 NRSV

"Jesus, Our Lord said, "Very Truly, I tell you, if you ask anything of the Father in my name, he will give it to you. Until now you have not asked for anything in my name. Ask and you will receive, so that your joy may be complete." John 16: 23a-24 NRSV

"Jesus, Our Lord said, 'Ask and it will be given you; search and you will find, knock, and the door will be opened for you. For everyone who asks receives, and everyone who searches finds, and for everyone who knocks, the door will be opened.'" Matthew 7: 7-8 NRSV

"Saint Paul, the apostle said, 'For this reason, since the day we heard it, we have not ceased praying for you and asking that you may be filled with the knowledge of God's will in all spiritual wisdom and understanding.'" Colossians 1: 9 NRSV

"Saint Paul, the apostle said, "First of all, I urge that supplications, prayers, intercessions, and thanksgivings be made for everyone, for kings and all who are in high positions, so that we may lead a quiet and peaceable life in all godliness and dignity.'" 1 Timothy 2: 1-2 NRSV

"Saint Paul, the apostle said, 'Likewise, the Spirit helps us in our weakness: for we do not know how to pray as we ought, but that very spirit intercedes with sighs too deep for words.'" Romans 8: 26 NRSV

PREFACE

This prayer book was written to help each of us grow in our faith in God. Prayer is our way of communication with God by telling him our needs and concerns and asking him for his blessings and help.

Some of us may have difficulty in praying to God. We may not know about God, who he is or what he stands for.

In John chapter 15, verse 14-15, Jesus talked about being friends with all. We can think that God is our friend and that we can talk to God as our friend.

Bringing prayer into our everyday lives will begin to add love, faith, and compassion into our inner-most thought processes. Gentleness, humbleness, and peace will surround the entirety of our lives, allowing our minds to reflect our goodness and knowledge onto others. Think about praying to God as you are being guided to pray. Remember, the more one prays to God, the nearer and closer one becomes to God.

The prayers in this book are meant to serve as a guide in providing direction in our daily prayers to the God.

Day 1

Oh Lord, I pray that

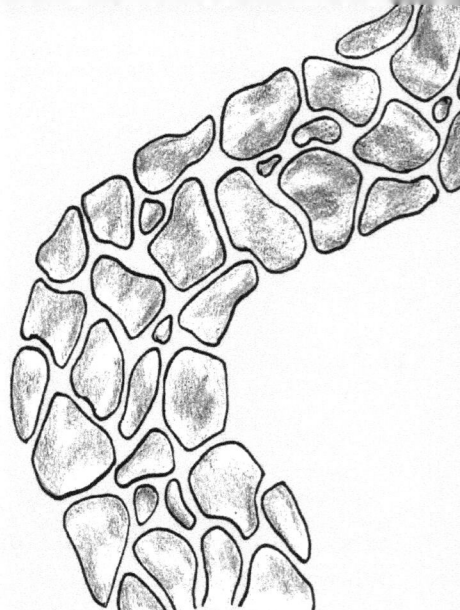

As I come to you this day, you will direct your spirit upon my path to show me the way that I should go. Help me to know that you are here with me, step by step, to guide and direct me as I face the challenges of another day. Surround me with your love and give me courage to do all that I need to do. Help me to trust that inner voice as your way of directing me in my life today, in your name, Oh Lord, I pray.

"And when you turn to the right or when you turn to the left, your ears shall hear a word behind you saying, 'This is the way; walk in it.'" Isaiah 30: 21 NRSV

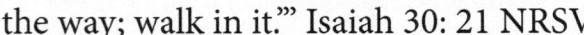

OH LORD I PRAY

Day 2

Oh Lord, I pray that

You will restore my soul from the depths of despair that I have been feeling. Help me Oh Lord, to get beyond this place of gloom and despair. Surround me with your love and compassion, and lift up my spirits to new heights, in your name, Oh Lord, I pray.

"Then they cried to the Lord in their trouble, and he brought them out from their distress; he made the storm be still, and the waves of the sea were hushed. Then they were glad because they had quiet, and he brought them to their desired haven." Psalm 107: 28-30 NRSV

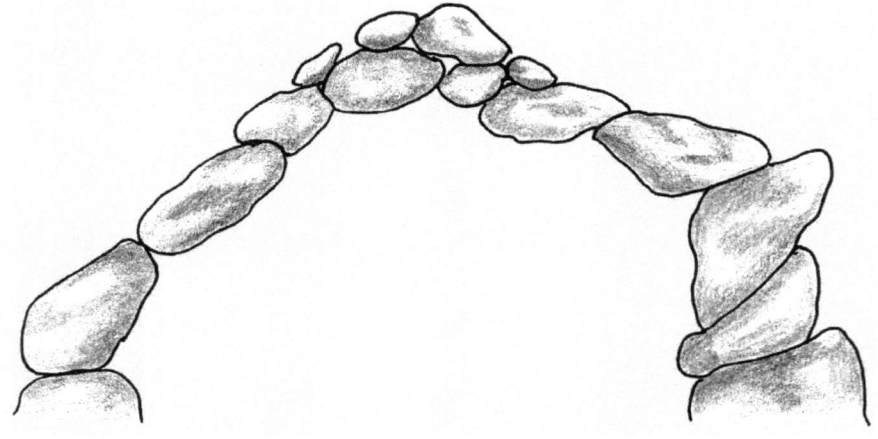

OH LORD I PRAY

Day 3

Oh Lord, I pray that

You will help me to become a good and faithful servant to you. Oh Lord, as I read your Word and pray to you, open my inner-most being to your knowledge and wisdom so that I may be a better servant to you by learning and following your ways. Help me, Oh Lord, to show love and compassion to all I come in contact with, I pray in your name.

"O the depth of the riches and wisdom and knowledge of God! How unsearchable are his judgments and how inscrutable his ways." Romans 11:33 NRSV

OH LORD I PRAY

Day 4

Oh Lord, I pray that

You will be with me this day. Surround me with your love and mercy and show me the right path to follow, the right decision to make. Oh Lord, I pray for your spirit to surround me this day, leading, guiding and directing me in your name I pray.

"I will instruct you and teach you the way you should go; I will counsel you with my eye upon you." Psalm 32:8 NRSV

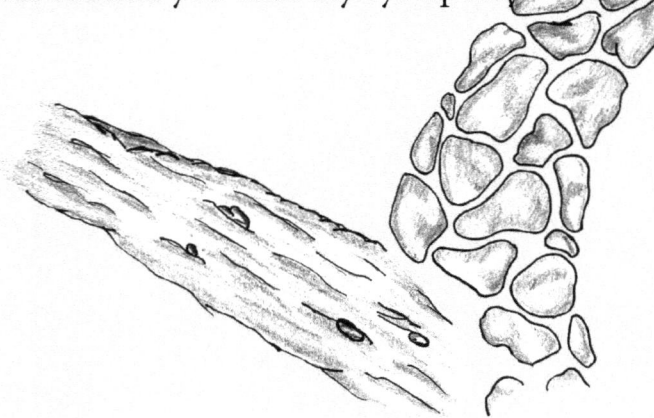

OH LORD I PRAY

Day 5

Oh Lord, I pray that

You will bring comfort to me today. My inner-most being is being confronted with the harsh truths and realities of life. Drive from me the fears and sorrows that I am facing and surround me with your love and compassion. Bring comfort to me, Oh Lord, in your name, I pray.

"Jesus, our Lord said, 'Come to me all you that are weary and are carrying heavy burdens, and I will give you rest. Take my yoke upon you, and learn from me; for I am gentle and humble in heart, and you will find rest for your souls. For my yoke is easy, and my burden is light.'" Matthew 11:28-29 NRSV

OH LORD I PRAY

Day 6

Oh Lord, I pray that

You will help me to place my trust in your will for me and my life. Lord, it is hard to accept the losses and hurts that occur in this life. Help me to look to you during these distressing times and realize that you are fulfilling your greater plan for me in this world in your name, Oh Lord, I pray.

"For surely I know the plans I have for you, says the Lord, plans for your welfare and not for harm to give you a future with hope." Jeremiah 29:11 NRSV

OH LORD I PRAY

Day 7

Oh Lord, I pray that

You will keep me from all self-righteousness and prideful thinking. Help me not to be critical or judgmental towards my loved ones and peers. Cleanse my soul of these destructive habits and create in me a loving and compassionate spirit, in your name, Oh Lord, I pray.

"Jesus, Our Lord said, 'Do not judge, so that you may not be judged. For with the judgement you make you will be judged, and the measure you give will be the measure you get.'" Matthew 7:1-2 NRSV

OH LORD I PRAY

Day 8

Oh Lord, I pray that

I will always be thankful for your blessings. Help me to be grateful for the many personal blessings you have given to me and for the opportunities that you have given to me. Oh Lord, you have opened many doors for me, allowing me to advance through my life bestowing me with blessings untold. In your name, Oh Lord, I pray that you will help me to always be thankful to you for all that you have done for me.

"Enter his gates with thanksgiving, and his courts with praise. Give thanks to him, bless his name." Psalm 100:4 NRSV

OH LORD I PRAY

Day 9

Oh Lord, I pray that

As I come to you today, you will let your spirit flow through my inner-most being, quenching that inner thirst you have placed in my soul for your knowledge and wisdom. Open my mind to your wisdom so that I may show discernment in serving you in your name, Oh Lord, I pray.

"If any of you is lacking in wisdom, ask God, who gives to all generously and ungrudgingly, and it will be given you." James 1:5 NRSV

OH LORD I PRAY

Day 10

Oh Lord, I pray that

I will place you first in my life, in all that I do. As I worship you, help me to remember the immensity of you, the greatness of your power, your everlasting love and mercy. Oh Lord, you are the Mighty One, all powerful and omnipotent, in full control. Help me Lord, to think of you as my first thought in the morning and my last thought at night; and to know your presence with me throughout today, as I strive to place you first in my life, in your name, Oh Lord, I pray.

"...for I am God, and there is no other; I am God and there is no one like me, declaring the end from the beginning and from ancient time things not yet done, saying, 'My purpose shall stand, and I will fulfill my intention,'" Isaiah 46:9 b-10 NRSV

OH LORD I PRAY

Day 11

Oh Lord, I pray that

As I come to you today as your servant, you will bring Christ's healing in Christ's name to this person I am serving. Surround this person with your eternal power and spirit, strengthening this person with your love and compassion, restoring and healing this person in your name, Oh Lord, I pray.

"For I will restore health to you, and your wounds I will heal, says the Lord." Jeremiah 30:17a NRSV

OH LORD I PRAY

Day 12

Oh Lord, I pray that

You will bring peace and comfort to this world of weary sufferers, opening pathways of thought and wisdom for each to know your way and direction. Help them to know that you are with them in their sufferings. Lord, you have suffered all pain, mockery and betrayal, degrading your humanity to the depths of the oceans, and yet, you showed us through your suffering how you overcame death through your resurrection. Oh Lord, I pray for your comfort and peace for these weary sufferers, in your name.

"Jesus, our Lord said, 'Peace I leave with you; my peace I give to you…Do not let your hearts be troubled, and do not let them be afraid.'" John 14:27 a-c NRSV

OH LORD I PRAY

Day 13

Oh Lord, I pray that

As I suffer from this hurt that is occurring in my life, you will surround me with your comfort and love. Lord, in my suffering, I look to you for help. Bring comfort to me. And help me to overcome my hurt and pain, restoring and healing my soul, in your name, Oh Lord, I pray.

"I have seen their ways, but I will heal them; I will lead them and repay them with comfort" …… Isaiah 57: 18 NRSV

OH LORD I PRAY

Day 14

Oh Lord, I pray that

You will give me the strength to overcome my many weaknesses. Lord, I am proud, vain, arrogant and selfish. Forgive me, oh Lord, from having these selfish traits. Help me to know when I am being selfish and self-centered and lead me from these selfish traits into your kingdom of service and love for others, in your name, Oh Lord, I pray.

"Rather, your iniquities have been barriers between you and your God, and your sins have hidden his face from you so that he does not hear." Isaiah 59:2 NRSV

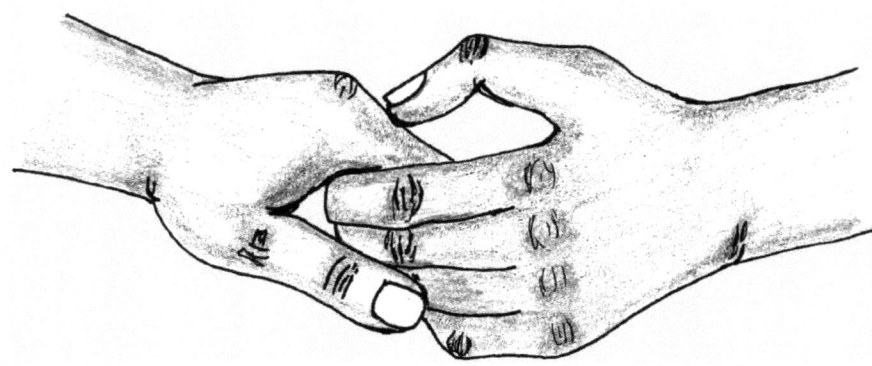

OH LORD I PRAY

Day 15

Oh Lord, I pray that

As I seek to be your servant, you will help me to penetrate those barriers that keep others from knowing you. Bring together differences in loving and peaceful surroundings, opening pathways of acceptance and understandings that come from your guidance and direction, in your name, Oh Lord, I pray.

"Now I appeal to you, brothers and sisters, by the name of our Lord Jesus Christ, that all you be in agreement and that there be no divisions among you, but that you be united in the same mind and the same purpose. 1st Corinthians 1:10 NRSV

OH LORD I PRAY

Day 16

Oh Lord, I pray that

In all that I do with my life today, I will not hinder another from coming to know you or hinder any relationship of one to you. Help me to be a witness for you through all that I do. If it be thy will, help me to bring one to you, for as you said in your word, one that is lost but now is found, brings more joy than the righteous ninety-nine, in your name, Oh Lord, I pray.

"Let us therefore no longer pass judgement on one another, but resolve instead never to put a stumbling block or hindrance in the way of another." Romans 14:13 NRSV

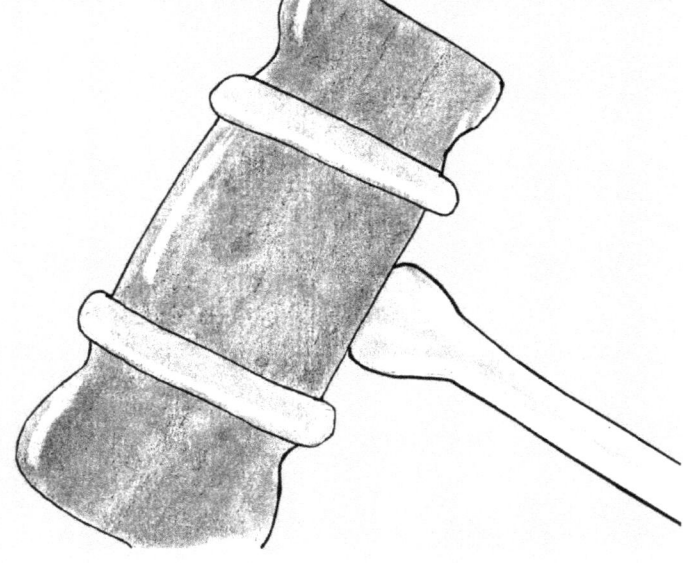

OH LORD I PRAY

Day 17

Oh Lord, I pray that

As I come to you today, you will take my hand and lead me into your presence. Surround me with your love and peace. Touch my thoughts with your guiding light, leading me into pathways of goodness and mercy, in your name, Oh Lord I pray.

"You show me the path of life. In your presence is fullness of joy. In your right hand are pleasures forevermore." Psalm 16, 11 NRSV

OH LORD I PRAY

Day 18

Oh Lord, I pray that

As your spirit flows through the depths of my soul to the fringes of my being, you will help me to touch another's soul with your love, peace, joy and gentleness. As you have shown your love to me, Oh Lord I pray in your name, to be a witness of that love to others. Help me to know the depth and width of that love; and to extend that love through thought or action to all that I come in contact with, in your name, Oh Lord, I pray.

"Above all, clothe yourselves with love, which binds everything together in perfect harmony. And let the peace of Christ rule in your hearts…" Colossians 3: 14-15a NRSV

OH LORD I PRAY

Day 19

Oh Lord, I pray that

In the stillness of my soul, I will feel your presence, in silence, I will know you are with me. That glow of light in my inner-most-being is your presence. The pure joy of your closeness is the highest feeling of spiritual exaltation possible in your name, Oh Lord I pray.

"For God alone my soul waits in silence, from him comes my salvation. He alone is my rock and salvation, my fortress; I shall never be shaken." Psalm 62, 1-2 NRSV

OH LORD I PRAY

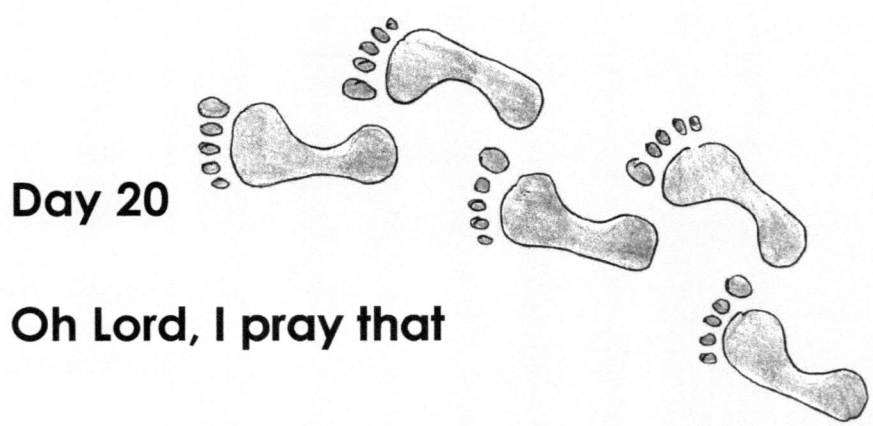

Day 20

Oh Lord, I pray that

As I grow in the knowledge of you, I will further understand your will for me. Help me, Oh Lord, not to impose my will onto others as I come before you with my prayers, Help me to trust you and to put my faith in you and your will for me and others, in your name, Oh Lord, I pray.

"Teach me to do your will, for you are my God. Let your good spirit lead me on a level path." Psalm 143:10 NRSV

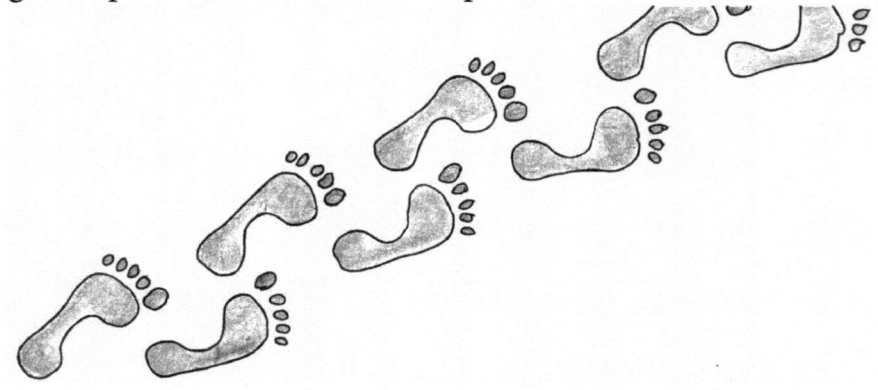

OH LORD I PRAY

Day 21

Oh Lord, I pray that

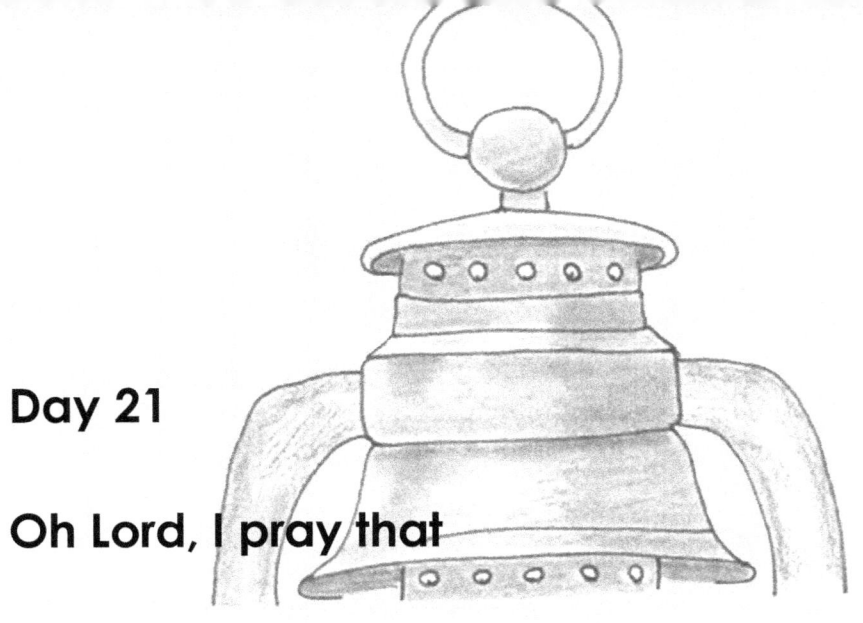

As I face the trials of today, you will surround me with your power and spirit. Guide me from these paths of darkness into your everlasting light, giving me strength and courage to face these challenges today, Oh Lord, in your name I pray.

"…as in the days when God watched over me; When his lamp shone over my head, and by his light I walked through darkness." Job 29:2b-3 NRSV

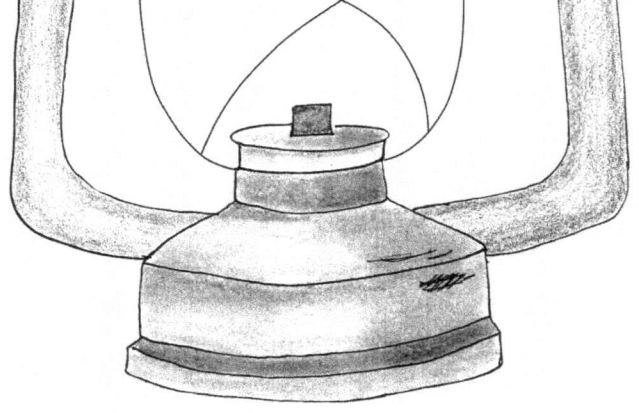

OH LORD I PRAY

Day 22

Oh Lord, I pray that

You will bring me into your presence. To know you, to sit at your table, to touch your garment, to feel the touch of your hand, is my everlasting longing. In your name, Oh Lord, I pray that you will quench this thirst with a flow of your living spirit into my inner-most being, drawing me closer and closer to you.

"Who shall ascend the hill of the Lord? And who shall stand in his holy place? Those who have clean hands and pure hearts, who do not lift up their souls to what is false, and do not swear what is false. Such is the company of those who seek him, who seek the face of the God of Jacob." Psalm 24:3, 4, 6 NRSV

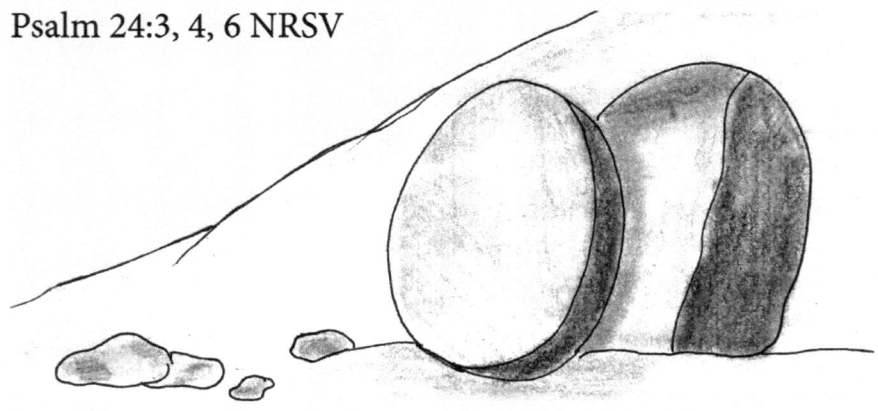

OH LORD I PRAY

Day 23

Oh Lord, I pray that

You will lead me from temptation. Give me the strength and wisdom to depart from evil ways, knowing that one devious thought can lead me down the wrong path. Bind up the tempter from me, Oh Lord, and direct my thoughts and ways into your will and purpose for me, Oh Lord, I pray in your name.

"Submit yourselves therefore to God, Resist the devil, and he will flee from you. Draw near to God and he will draw near to you...." James 4:7-8a NSRV

OH LORD I PRAY

Day 24

Oh Lord, I pray that

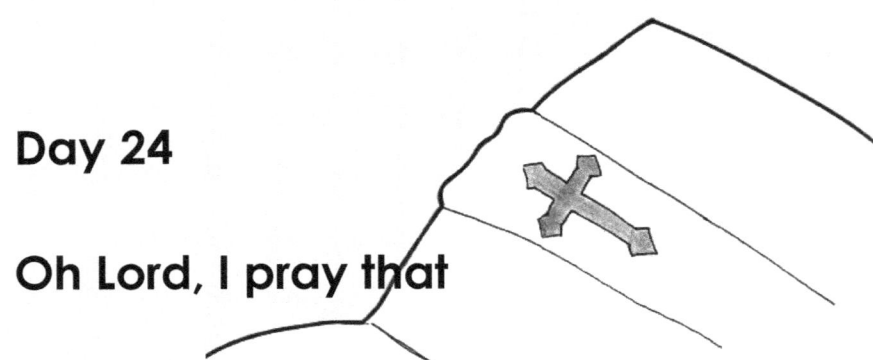

You will help me to pray for others. How often I come to you with my own burdens and needs, praying for myself and not thinking of others. Help me to think and pray for others, being sensitive to their needs and burdens, giving me understanding and acceptance, Oh Lord, I pray in your name.

"Do nothing from selfish ambition or conceit, but in humility regard others as better than yourselves. Let each of you look not to your own interests, but to the interests of others." Philippians 2: 3-4 NSRV

OH LORD I PRAY

Day 25

Oh Lord, I pray that

You will help me to do the best I can as I go about my daily living. Oh Lord, at times, circumstances seem overwhelming, with time and events becoming more stressful and complicated. Help me to know what is important and guide me in my decision-making as I face these challenges, in your name, I pray, Oh Lord.

"Trust in the Lord with all your heart, and do not rely on your own insight. In all your ways acknowledge him, and he will make straight your paths." Proverbs 3:5-6 NRSV

OH LORD I PRAY

Day 26

Oh Lord, I pray that

You will help me not to worry so much. I know, oh Lord, that if I will place my faith and trust in you, and you alone, I will not be overcome by these worrying thoughts. Strengthen my inner faith so that when worry enters my mind, I can push that fearful thought, that annoying, irritating fear from my mind, in your name, Oh Lord, I pray.

Jesus, our Lord said "Therefore I tell you, do not worry about your life, what you will eat or what you will drink, or about your body, what you will wear. Is not life more than food, and the body more than clothing? Look at the birds of the air; they neither sow nor reap nor gather into barns, and yet your heavenly Father feeds them. But if God so clothes the grass of the field, ...will he not much more clothe you...Therefore, do not worry." Matthew 6 25-26;31-31a NSRV

OH LORD I PRAY

Day 27

Oh Lord, I pray that

You will help me not to be self-serving and striving for self-gain… Help me, Oh Lord, to direct my ambitious nature away from self-gain and self-glory to serving you and your kingdom, glorifying and exalting you. Take that greedy desire for self-gain to the depths of the oceans, Oh Lord, I pray in your name.

"But those who want to be rich fall into temptation and are trapped by many senseless and harmful desires that plunge people into ruin and destruction. For the love of money is a root of all kinds of evil, and in their eagerness to be rich some have wandered away from the faith and pierced themselves with many pains." Timothy 6: 9-10 NRSV

OH LORD I PRAY

Day 28

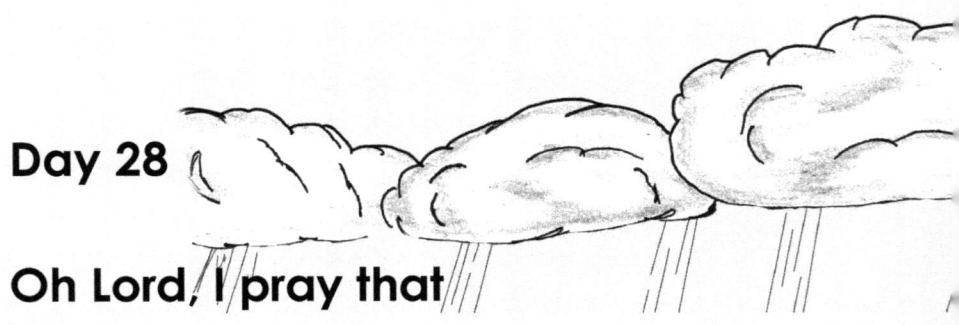

Oh Lord, I pray that

You will help me to glorify you and exalt you in all that I do. Help me, oh Lord, not to seek self-glory when I am serving you. Lead me from all self-glory to glorifying you in all that I do, in your name, Oh Lord, I pray.

"Jesus, Our Lord said, '...let your light shine before others, so that they may see your good works and give glory to your Father in heaven.'" Matthew 5:16b NRSV

OH LORD I PRAY

Day 29

Oh Lord, I pray that

You will be with this one, my friend, who seems so alone and confused; lost and wondering without direction. Bring my friend into your throne room so that he will get to know you and serve you. Open my friend's mind, giving him insight into your knowledge and ways, bringing peace and comfort, in your name, Oh Lord, I pray.

"Do not fear, for I am with you, do not be afraid, for I am your God; I will strengthen you, I will help you, I will uphold you with my victorious right hand." Isaiah 41:10 NRSV

OH LORD I PRAY

Day 30

Oh Lord, I pray that

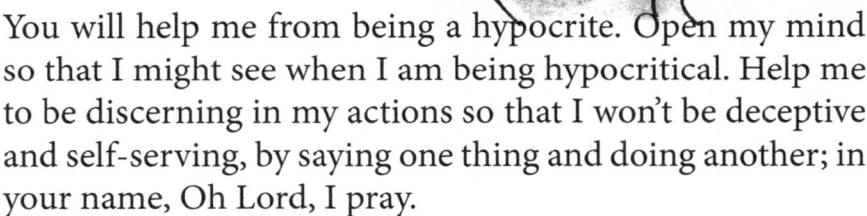

You will help me from being a hypocrite. Open my mind so that I might see when I am being hypocritical. Help me to be discerning in my actions so that I won't be deceptive and self-serving, by saying one thing and doing another; in your name, Oh Lord, I pray.

"Jesus, Our Lord said '…but do not do as they do, for they do not practice what they teach." Matthew 23:3b NRSV

OH LORD I PRAY

Day 31

Oh Lord, I pray that

I can come to you as your humble servant, drawing nearer to you, exalting and glorifying your name. Help me, Oh Lord, to be an example to others so that they may learn to know and love you, in your name, Oh Lord, I pray.

Jesus, Our Lord said, "Go into all the world and proclaim the good news to the whole creation." Mark 16:15 b. NRSV

OH LORD I PRAY

www.ingramcontent.com/pod-product-compliance
Lightning Source LLC
LaVergne TN
LVHW050137080526
838202LV00061B/6506